G000122706

I DON'T MEAN TO MEAN TO BE RUDE, BUT...

ICE HOUSE BOOKS

Published by Ice House Books

Copyright © 2020 Ice House Books

Written by Rebecca Du Pontet
Designed by Kayleigh Hudson

Ice House Books is an imprint of Half Moon Bay Limited
The Ice House, 124 Walcot Street, Bath, BA1 5BG
www.icehousebooks.co.uk

ISBN 978-1-912867-35-6

Printed in China

TO:

_____

FROM:

_____

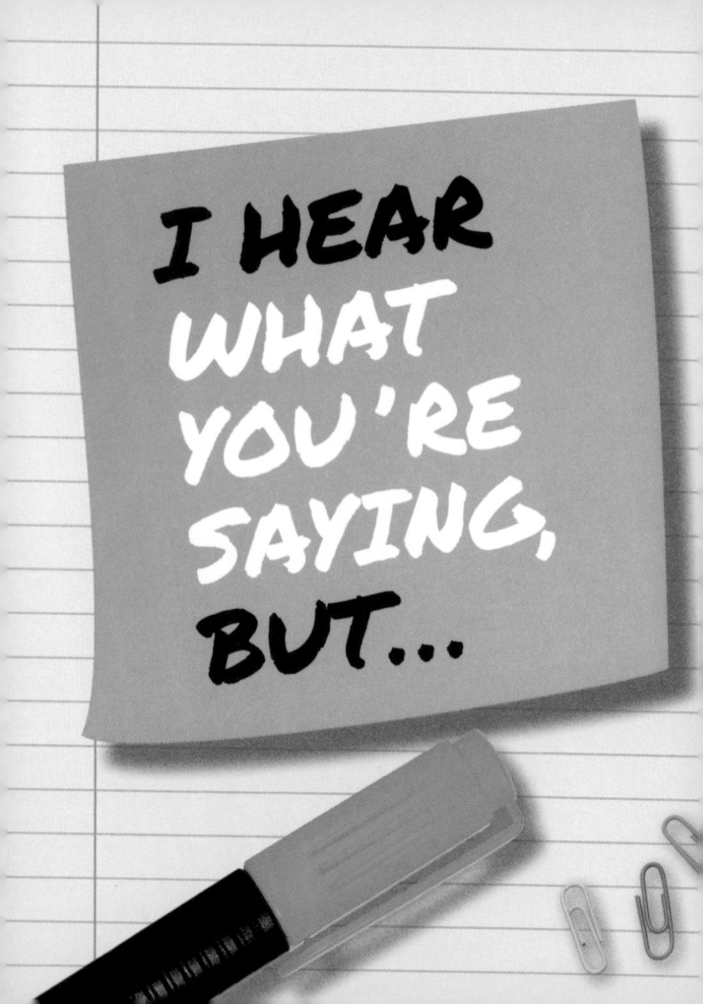
I HEAR
WHAT
YOU'RE
SAYING,
BUT...

WHAT THEY REALLY MEAN:

I hear you — as in your vocals have reached my inner ears — but I choose to ignore every single last word of it, because you are WRONG.

WHAT THEY REALLY MEAN:

TBH I switched off after the first minute of your moan-ologue. I have literally no idea what you are on about, but I'll play along until it becomes clear or I can extricate myself from this conversation.

I DON'T MEAN TO BE RUDE, BUT...

WHAT THEY REALLY MEAN:

I'm about to be really rude — it's what I set out to do and now I am going to do it, blatantly, unapologetically, in your face.

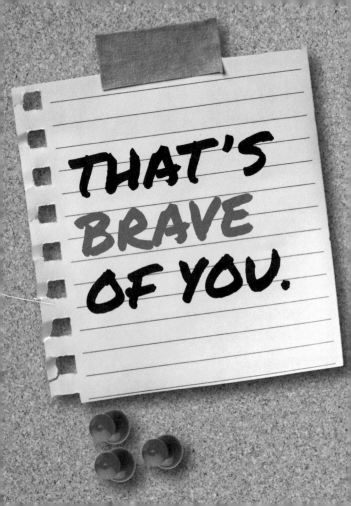

WHAT THEY REALLY MEAN:

This is going to be the most arrogant thing I've ever said, and it is definitely not my place to say it, but I will say it, nevertheless.

WHAT THEY REALLY MEAN:

I'm not interested,
I will never be interested,
and I think you are talking
a load of old codswallop.

I'm just talking to
you till someone
genuinely interesting
comes along.

WHAT THEY REALLY MEAN:

I've been wanting to say something for days/weeks/years, and I am getting some serious enjoyment from watching your face recoil in horror. Man, I feel sooo much better!

DON'T
WORRY,
IT'S NOT
IMPORTANT.

WHAT THEY REALLY MEAN:

It IS important, but I don't have time for you to get your head around it and I wish I hadn't started this conversation. I'll ask someone else.

WHAT THEY REALLY MEAN:

That has got to be one of the worst things I've heard, but I literally cannot think of anything else to say. I hope this will be enough to make you feel better and we can move on.

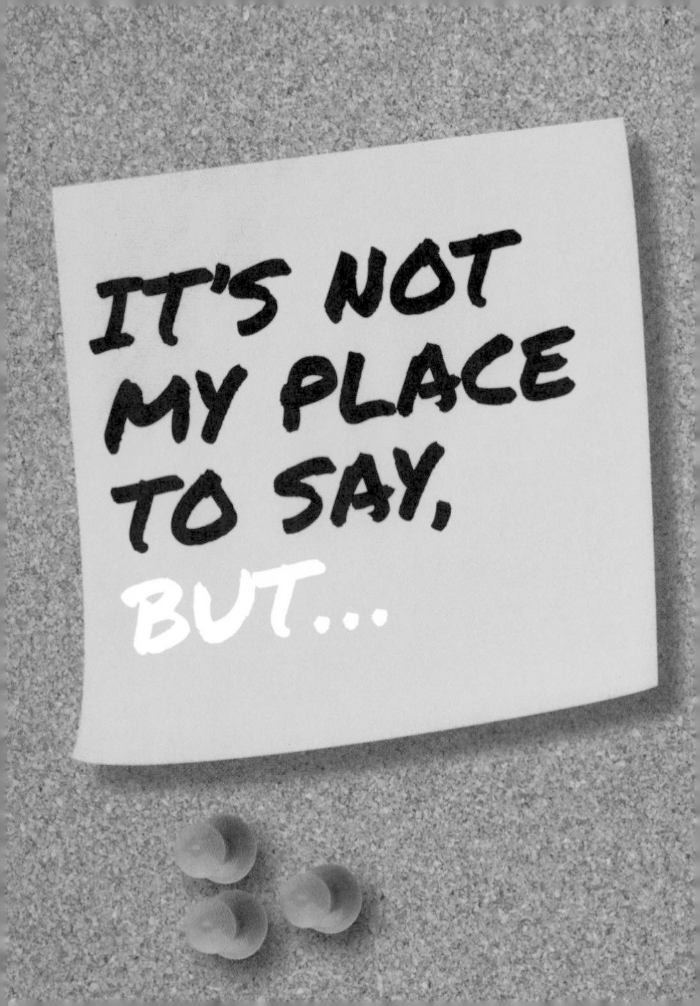
IT'S NOT
MY PLACE
TO SAY,
BUT...

WHAT THEY REALLY MEAN:

I <u>absolutely</u> think it's my place to say, even if no one else agrees. You're going to hear me out anyway, so listen up.

WHAT THEY REALLY MEAN:

I'm not even vaguely sorry, otherwise I wouldn't have barged in like this and started talking over you. What I have to say is more important. Listen to me instead.

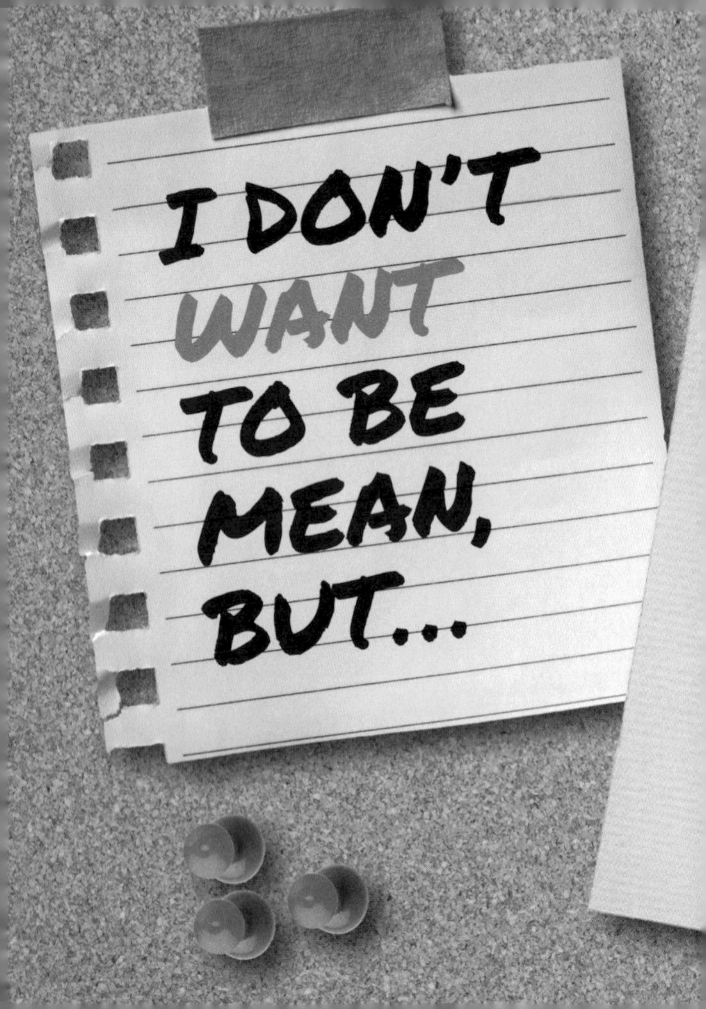
I DON'T
WANT
TO BE
MEAN,
BUT...

WHAT THEY REALLY MEAN:

What I'm going to say is really savage, but I'm trying to sugar-coat it by pretending I'm not as mean as I actually am. Someone needs a reality check and I'm going to give it to them, both barrels.

YOU MUST
DO WHAT
FEELS
RIGHT
FOR YOU...

WHAT THEY REALLY MEAN:

Rather you than me.
Boy is it going to bite you
in the a*se, because it is
THE WRONG DECISION!!
But I'll just leave you to
carry on with your blatant
self-flagellation while I go off
and make a cup of tea.

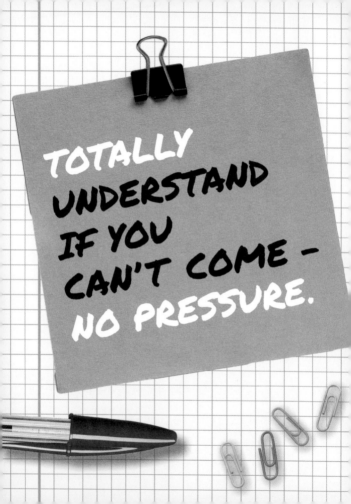

WHAT THEY REALLY MEAN:

On your head be it.

You know the right choice here, but I don't have time to try and convince you otherwise. In fact, it might be better if you don't come, now I'm thinking about it...

WHAT THEY REALLY MEAN:

I do mind.

I have never minded more about something in my entire godforsaken life. You know I mind, and you know what the correct decision is, so you had better make it.

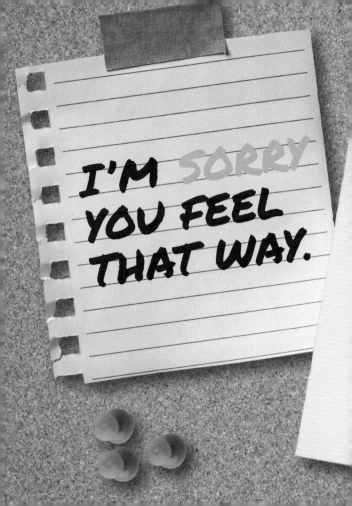

WHAT THEY REALLY MEAN:

You need to get over yourself. You're being irrational and, quite frankly, I don't give a tiny rat's a*se HOW you feel.

I'LL

BEAR

IT IN

MIND...

WHAT THEY REALLY MEAN:

I won't. I discounted your advice before you'd even finished giving it. I'll brush it away along with all the other useless opinions I receive. I know best, and that's the end of it.

WHAT THEY REALLY MEAN:

Ouch, that's some
seriously bad sh*t.
Like, SO bad. I actually
can't believe you've just
told me that, let alone
actually DONE it.

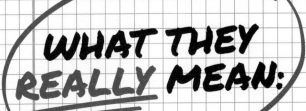

WHAT THEY REALLY MEAN:

I'm about to brutally attack your character and life decisions all in the name of 'advice'. I'm just being a good friend/helpful colleague/ stranger in a queue.

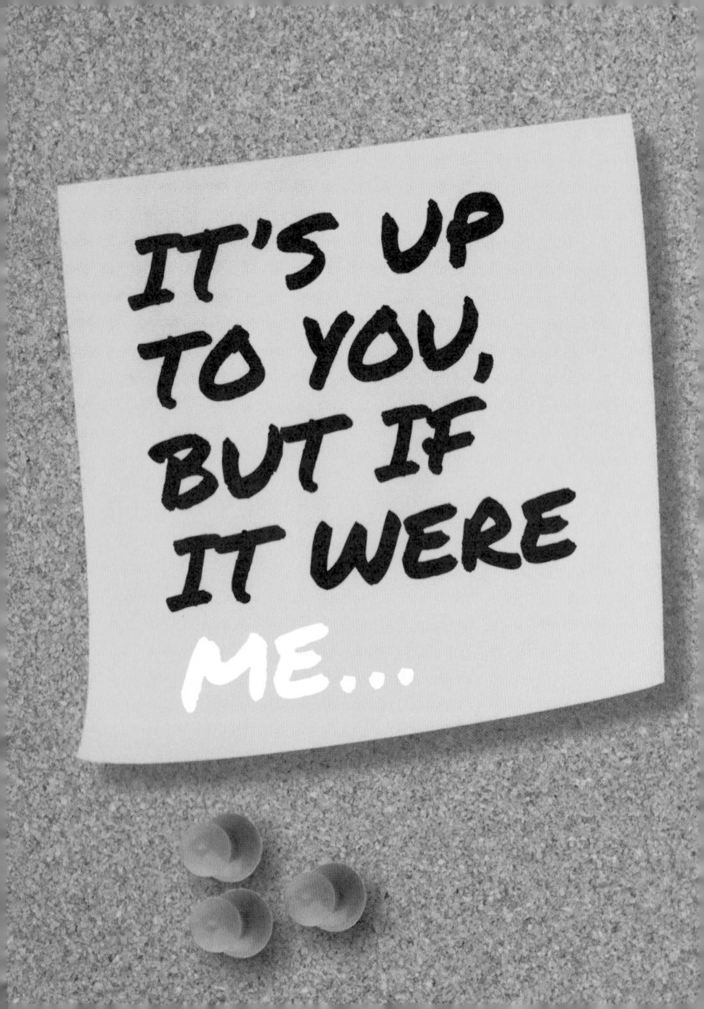
IT'S UP TO YOU, BUT IF IT WERE
ME...

WHAT THEY REALLY MEAN:

STOP!

You're making completely the wrong choice, and if you don't do what I advise you're probably beyond help anyway.

SURE, LET'S TALK SOON AND GET SOMETHING IN THE DIARY.

WHAT THEY REALLY MEAN:

I've run out of different ways to ask "how are things with you?" so am now moving on to totally insincere promises, which we'll both inevitably forget about, until the next time we bump into each other and go through this charade all over again ...

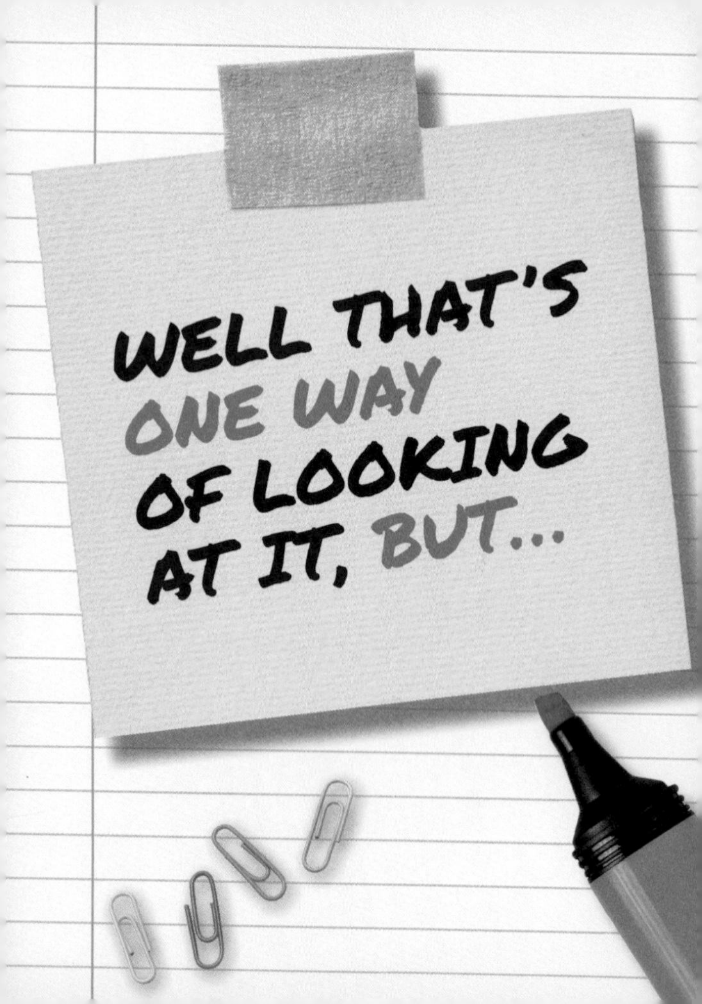
WELL THAT'S ONE WAY OF LOOKING AT IT, BUT...

WHAT THEY REALLY MEAN:

I don't agree at all.
You're being a
narrow-minded,
pig-headed zealot
and if you'd let me get
even one word in sideways,
you'd see things from my
perspective and realise
how wrong you truly are.

WHAT THEY REALLY MEAN:

You're going to be seriously offended by this, but I pre-empted my tirade with 'no offence', so you have no right to get annoyed by anything I say. OK?

WHAT THEY REALLY MEAN:

I've set this out to you very clearly a million times. Stop being an eejit, I haven't got time to explain again. Stop wasting my extremely precious time.

YOU
LOOK
TIRED...

WHAT THEY REALLY MEAN:

OMG, you look dreadful. Really awful. What happened? You're going to need to sleep non-stop for a week to look alive again.

WHAT THEY REALLY MEAN:

I'm about to 'suggest' you do the complete opposite of what you've just told me. I've been waiting to interrupt from the moment you opened your mouth. You're hurting my head.

WHAT THEY REALLY MEAN:

It's totally your fault, but I'm taking the blame to (a) end the conversation and (b) gain the upper hand, by appearing to be a really lovely, humble, sickeningly likeable person.

YOU'RE
LUCKY
YOU CAN
DO THAT...

WHAT THEY REALLY MEAN:

I am insanely jealous of your low-stress, lazy-arsed life. Some of us have to WORK FOR A LIVING, FIVE WHOLE DAYS A WEEK you know.

WHAT THEY REALLY MEAN:

I don't like your idea at all. In fact, this is probably some of the worst work I have ever seen. Start from scratch, do better or get out.

WHAT THEY REALLY MEAN:

I am giving you absolutely zero respect. End of. (Probably followed by a blatant insult or unsolicited advice, possibly bad news, delivered in an extremely insensitive and brash fashion.)

WHAT THEY REALLY MEAN:

I'm not sure I even know what I mean, but if I use this precursor it may
(a) lend what I'm going to say some kind of plausibility and
(b) buy me some time while I work out what it is I actually really mean.

WHAT THEY REALLY MEAN:

We both know there is absolutely no way I'm joining you later. I'm already planning on going home, getting straight into my PJs, eating fast food and binge-watching boxsets.

(Must. Stop. Lying.)

I
PERSONALLY
FEEL...

WHAT THEY REALLY MEAN:

OK, what I'm about to do here is to slap down every thought you've ever had, or made the mistake of uttering out loud, all in the name of honesty. (Don't even get us started on the unnecessary use of the adverb 'personally' — the pronoun 'I' will do just fine.)

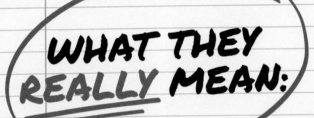

WHAT THEY REALLY MEAN:

It IS you,
it's always been you —
you are so wrong for me,
it hurts, and you were
only ever a stand-in until
someone better came along.
And now they have,
so bye-bye.

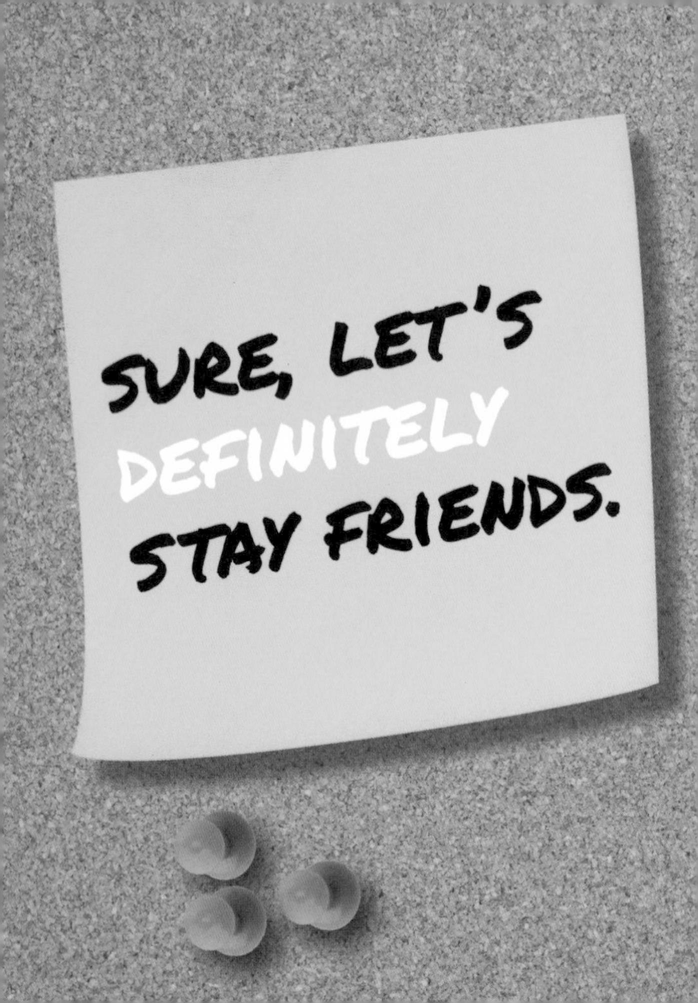
SURE, LET'S
DEFINITELY
STAY FRIENDS.

WHAT THEY REALLY MEAN:

I am a bare-faced liar.
There is no way on earth
we are staying friends –
never were, never gonna be.
See – deleting your number
as I'm walking away, quickly.

FEEL
FREE TO
JOIN US.

WHAT THEY REALLY MEAN:

You're weren't top
of the list, but I'm inviting
you now as an afterthought
in case you hear about
it on the grapevine/
Facebook/Instagram.

WHAT THEY REALLY MEAN:

I'm desperately trying to think of something meaningful to say. What was the question again? Hang on, was there a question?

(Beloved by football pundits, this inane and clichéd phrase is probably one of the worst offenders in our list of crimes against language.)

SURE, YOU
SHOULD DO
WHAT YOU
LOVE.

WHAT THEY REALLY MEAN:

Lovely pipe dream, but unless you have a secret trust fund, it's never going to happen — on account of you needing to pay the rent/mortgage/bailiffs.

WHAT THEY REALLY MEAN:

I'm using this meaningless phrase as an out-and-out stalling tactic to fend you off for a bit longer, until you give up.

(Those who utter this are barely disguised harbingers of DOOM, ready to wreck your hopes and dreams at a moment's notice.)

IT IS
WHAT
IT IS...

WHAT THEY REALLY MEAN:

I'm madly prevaricating, scrabbling around for something useful/ meaningful/vaguely half-intelligent to say, and this was the best I could come up with.

(We'll tell you what it is — it's lazy and annoying.)

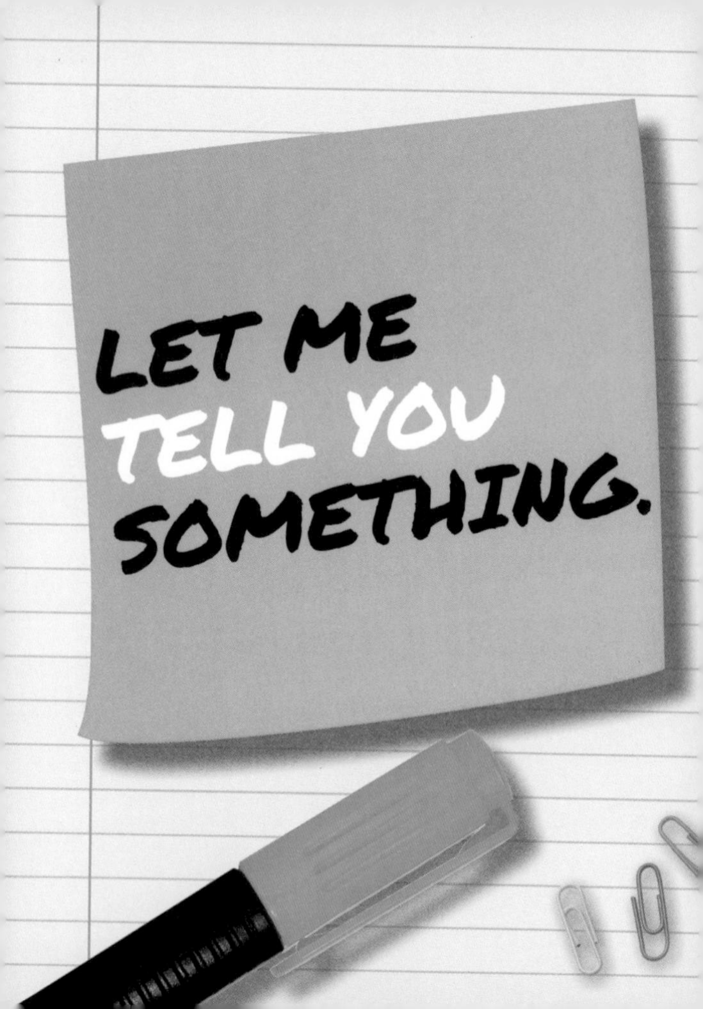
LET ME
TELL YOU
SOMETHING.

WHAT THEY REALLY MEAN:

I'm about to impart some sort of sanctimonious, self-serving, irrelevant piece of advice, which you WILL listen to.

(You know what, NO — we won't let you tell us something.)

WHAT THEY REALLY MEAN:

Watch out!
I'm either about to be
staggeringly dishonest
or horribly insulting.
Actually, on second
thoughts, probably both.

I'M
SORRY
YOU'RE
UPSET BY
WHAT I
SAID...

WHAT THEY REALLY MEAN:

I'm not in the slightest bit sorry. I stand by what I said. TBH I think you're being pathetic.

(Offenders — you know full well that this is a feeble attempt at a meaningless apology — the epitome of #sorrynotsorry.)

WHAT THEY REALLY MEAN:

Do as I say or prepare
to meet your maker. I am
being polite (for the
moment at least),
but we both know the
subtext here, loud and clear
— do what I've asked, or
repent in your own time.

I SEE WHAT YOU'RE GETTING AT...

WHAT THEY REALLY MEAN:

I see what you're getting at and I don't like it one little bit. However, I'll attempt (through gritted teeth) to keep things civilised for a bit longer for the sake of those around us.

WHAT THEY REALLY MEAN:

I don't really have an opinion on this topic, but I so badly want to say something, *anything,* to get involved in the conversation, alongside a need for all concerned to realise what a thoroughly decent person I am.

(Culprits are often referred to as 'fence dwellers'.)

WHAT THEY REALLY MEAN:

I'm making a ham-fisted attempt to avoid coming across as patronising about things you may or may not know, and in doing so, I am actually making myself sound like an absolute t*t.

(Just. Don't. Say it.)

THAT'S ALL VERY WELL
BUT...

Pay attention! I'm about to sound off, VERY LOUDLY, about my deeply divisive theories on politics, life, death and anything else I can get my teeth into.

WHAT THEY REALLY MEAN:

I'm about to be overwhelmingly rude and officious with you, either until we come to blows or you drag your sorry a*se away somewhere to lick your wounds.

WHAT THEY REALLY MEAN:

I totally lost the thread of this conversation ten minutes ago. I'm thoroughly confused and need to try and remember the main point. Give me a minute...

WHAT THEY REALLY MEAN:

I am really important and like nothing more than leaning way back in my chair and talking in this smug, self-satisfied way about nothing at all because I'm incredibly, nauseatingly pleased with myself.

(No surprise then that this is a phrase vastly overused by boorish politicians.)

WHAT THEY REALLY MEAN:

This is just something pointless I tag onto the end of my sentences to imply some kind of (non-existent) shared experiences/opinions/history. Know what I mean?

IT'S ALL GOOD...

(HINT: IT RARELY IS)

WHAT THEY REALLY MEAN:

The last thing it is is good. In fact, it's a total sh*tshow, but let's carry on regardless and smile through the pain and embarrassment.

PHOTO CREDITS